Selected Translations

Leo Yankevich

ANCIENT CYPRESS PRESS
Fort Lauderdale

BOOKS BY LEO YANKEVICH

Collections
The Unfinished Crusade
The Last Silesian
Tikkun Olam (Second Edition)
Journey Late At Night

Chapbooks
The Language of Birds
Grief's Herbs (after Stanisław Grochowiak)
The Gnosis of Gnomes
Epistle from the Dark
The Golem of Gleiwitz

E-Books
Metaphysics
"You Who Live and Hear"
Tikkun Olam (First Edition)

Ancient Cypress Press
Fort Lauderdale
Florida, USA
www.ancientcypresspress.com

Copyright © 2013 Ancient Cypress Press

All rights reserved—no part of this book may be reproduced in any form without permission in writing from the publisher, except by a reviewer who wishes to quote brief passages in connection with a review in a magazine or newspaper.

ISBN: 978-0-9889648-3-9

ACKNOWLEDGEMENTS

Some of these translations have appeared in the following publications, to whose editors I offer grateful acknowledgement:

Chronicles, Counter Currents, Iambs & Trochees, The New Formalist, Trinacria, The Sarmatian Review, & The Susquehanna Quarterly

CONTENTS

STEPY AKERMAŃSKIE	10
THE AKKERMAN STEPPE	11
CISZA MORSKA	12
THE CALM OF THE SEA	13
RUINY ZAMKU W BAŁAKŁAWIE	14
THE CASTLE RUINS AT BALAKLAVA	15
CZATYRDACH	16
CHATYR DAH	17
ПАРУС	18
THE SAIL	19
СОН	20
THE DREAM	21
PRZESZŁOŚĆ	22
THE PAST	23
ARCHAISCHER TORSO APOLLOS	24
APOLLO'S ARCHAIC TORSO	25
CHWILA	26
THE MOMENT	27

ASTERN	28
ASTERS	29
LETZTER FRÜHLING	30
LAST SPRING	31
EIN HERBSTABEND	32
AN AUTUMN EVENING	33
НОЧЬ	34
NIGHT	35
БЕРЕЗА	36
THE BIRCH	37
DEZEMBER 1942	38
DECEMBER 1942	39
ZABIJANIE RYBY	40
KILLING FISH	41
KOLĘDA	42
CAROL	43
CZARNE CZARNE GAWRONY	44
BLACK, BLACK ROOKS	45
NOTES ON THE POETS	47
A POEM BY LEO YANKEVICH	55
ABOUT LEO YANKEVICH	59

SELECTED TRANSLATIONS

STEPY AKERMAŃSKIE

Wpłynąłem na suchego przestwór oceanu,
Wóz nurza się w zieloność i jak łódka brodzi;
Śród fali łąk szumiących, śród kwiatów powodzi,
Omijam koralowe ostrowy burzanu.

Już mrok zapada, nigdzie drogi ni kurhanu,
Patrzę w niebo, gwiazd szukam, przewodniczek łodzi;
Tam z dala błyszczy obłok—tam jutrzenka wschodzi;
To błyszczy Dniestr, to weszła lampa Akermanu.

Stójmy!—jak cicho!—słyszę ciągnące żurawie,
Których by nie dościgły źrenice sokoła;
Słyszę, kędy się motyl kołysa na trawie,

Kędy wąż śliską piersią dotyka się zioła.
W takiej ciszy—tak ucho natężam ciekawie,
Że słyszałbym głos z Litwy.—Jedźmy, nikt nie woła.

— *Adam Mickiewicz (1798-1855)*

THE AKKERMAN STEPPE

I launch myself across the dry and open narrows,
My carriage plunging into green as if a ketch,
Floundering through the meadow flowers in the stretch.
I pass an archipelago of coral yarrows.

It's dusk now, not a road in sight, nor ancient barrows.
I look up at the sky and look for stars to catch.
There distant clouds glint—there tomorrow starts to etch;
The Dnieper glimmers; Akkerman's lamp shines and harrows.

I stand in stillness, hear the migratory cranes,
Their necks and wings beyond the reach of preying hawks;
Hear where the sooty copper glides across the plains,

Where on its underside a viper writhes through stalks.
Amid the hush I lean my ears down grassy lanes
And listen for a voice from home. Nobody talks.

—after the Polish of Adam Mickiewicz (1798-1855)

CISZA MORSKA
Na wysokości Tarkankut

Już wstążkę pawilonu wiatr zaledwie muśnie,
Cichymi gra piersiami rozjaśniona woda;
Jak marząca o szczęściu narzeczona młoda
Zbudzi się, aby westchnąć, i wnet znowu uśnie.

Żagle, na kształt chorągwi gdy wojnę skończono,
Drzemią na masztach nagich; okręt lekkim ruchem
Kołysa się, jak gdyby przykuty łańcuchem;
Majtek wytchnął, podróżne rozśmiało się grono.

O morze! pośród twoich wesołych żyjątek
Jest polip, co śpi na dnie, gdy się niebo chmurzy,
A na ciszę długimi wywija ramiony.

O myśli! w twojej głębi jest hydra pamiątek,
Co śpi wpośród złych losów i namiętnej burzy;
A gdy serce spokojne, zatapia w nim szpony.

— *Adam Mickiewicz (1798-1855)*

THE CALM OF THE SEA
Upon the height of Tarkankut

The pennant at the crow's nest rises with the breeze,
Shafts of sunlight play upon the water's breast
As on a bride-to-be who wakes to sigh and rest,
And wakes again and sighs for dreams that better please.

On naked spars the banner-shaped sails hang at ease.
The vessel is in chains now, leeside facing west,
Lulled by slow rocking. Passengers lampoon in jest,
Swabbies sigh to one another, slapping knees.

Blithe Sea! Among your jolly living creatures is
The polyp, sleeping in your depths when dark clouds swarm,
Wielding longish arms amid each starfish grave.

Sweet dreams! Below a hydra of remembrances
Sleeps in the middle of mishaps and raging storm,
And when the heart is calm, its pincers flash and wave.

—*after the Polish of Adam Mickiewicz (1798-1855)*

RUINY ZAMKU W BAŁAKŁAWIE

Te zamki, połamane zwaliska bez ładu,
Zdobiły cię i strzegły, o niewdzięczny Krymie!
Dzisiaj sterczą na górach jak czaszki olbrzymie,
W nich gad mieszka lub człowiek podlejszy od gadu.

Szczeblujmy na wieżycę! Szukam herbów śladu;
Jest i napis, tu może bohatera imię,
Co było wojsk postrachem, w zapomnieniu drzymie,
Obwinione jak robak liściem winogradu.

Tu Grek dłutował w murach ateńskie ozdoby,
Stąd Italczyk Mongołom narzucał żelaza
I mekkański przybylec nucił pieśń namaza.

Dziś sępy czarnym skrzydłem oblatują groby;
Jak w mieście, które całkiem wybije zaraza,
Wiecznie z baszt powiewają chorągwie żałoby.

—*Adam Mickiewicz (1798-1855)*

THE CASTLE RUINS AT BALAKLAVA

These castles, whose remains are strewn in heaps for miles,
Once graced and guarded you, Crimea the ungrateful!
Today they sit upon the hills, each like a great skull
In which reptiles reside or men worse than reptiles.

Let's climb a tower, search for crests upon worn tiles,
For an inscription or a hero's name, the fateful
Bane of armies now forgotten by the faithful,
A wizened beetle wrapped in vines below the aisles.

Here Greeks wrought Attic ornaments upon the walls,
From which Italians would cast Mongols into chains,
And where the Mecca-bound once stopped to pray and beg.

Today above the tombs the shadow of night falls,
The black-winged buzzards fly like pennants over plains,
As if towards a city ever touched by plague.

—*after the Polish of Adam Mickiewicz (1798-1855)*

CZATYRDACH

Drżąc muślemin całuje stopy twej opoki,
Maszcie krymskiego statku, wieki Czatyrdachu!
O minarecie świata! o gór padyszachu!
Ty, nad skały poziomu uciekłszy w obłoki,

Siedzisz sobie pod bramą niebios, jak wysoki
Gabryjel pilnujący edeńskiego gmachu;
Ciemny las twoim płaszczem, a janczary strachu
Twój turban z chmur haftują błyskawic potoki.

Nam czy słońce dopieka, czyli mgła ocienia,
Czy sarańcza plon zetnie, czy giaur pali domy -
Czatyrdachu, ty zawsze głuchy, nieruchomy,

Między światem i niebem jak drogman stworzenia,
Podesławszy pod nogi ziemie, ludzi, gromy,
Słuchasz tylko, co mówi Bóg do przyrodzenia.

—*Adam Mickiewicz (1798-1855)*

CHATYR DAH

The trembling Muslims kiss your foot and pray out loud,
O mast of the Crimean tall ship Chatyr Dah,
Minaret amid the hills and Padishah!
You, having fled above the cliffs into a cloud,

Stand at the gates of heaven, humbling the crowd,
And, like great Gabriel, guard lost Eden's house, your shaw
Of trees a cloak where janissaries keep the law,
Your turban thunderbolts and lightning for the proud.

And yet sun scolds our brows and fog obscures our ways,
Locusts poach our crops and Gavur burn our homes,
Always, Chatyr Dah, as motionless as domes

In Mecca, you remain indifferent to our days,
Creation's dragoman to what below you roams
Who only hears whatever God to nature says.

—after the Polish of Adam Mickiewicz (1798-1855)

ПАРУС

Белеет парус одинокой
В тумане моря голубом!..
Что ищет он в стране далекой?
Что кинул он в краю родном?..

Играют волны - ветер свищет,
И мачта гнется и скрипит...
Увы! он счастия не ищет
И не от счастия бежит!

Под ним струя светлей лазури,
Над ним луч солнца золотой...
А он, мятежный, просит бури,
Как будто в бурях есть покой!

—*Михаил Лермонтов (1814-1841)*

THE SAIL

A lonely sail moves, white on white,
Amid the ocean's mist and foam.
Caught now in a distant light,
What does it seek so far from home?

The halyards groan, the mast-beam creaks;
The sail now billows in the breeze.
It is not happiness it seeks,
Nor happiness from which it flees.

Above, the sun is blithe and warm;
Below, the blue waves rise and crest.
The rebel searches for a storm
As if in storms it could find rest.

—*after the Russian of Mikhail Lermontov (1814-1841)*

СОН

В полдневный жар в долине Дагестана
С свинцом в груди лежал недвижим я;
Глубокая еще дымилась рана,
По капле кровь точилася моя.

Лежал один я на песке долины;
Уступы скал теснилися кругом,
И солнце жгло их желтые вершины
И жгло меня - но спал я мертвым сном.

И снился мне сияющий огнями
Вечерний пир в родимой стороне.
Меж юных жен, увенчанных цветами,
Шел разговор веселый обо мне.

Но в разговор веселый не вступая,
Сидела там задумчиво одна,
И в грустный сон душа ее младая
Бог знает чем была погружена;

И снилась ей долина Дагестана;
Знакомый труп лежал в долине той;
В его груди, дымясь, чернела рана,
И кровь лилась хладеющей струей.

—*Михаил Лермонтов (1814-1841)*

THE DREAM

High noon in Dagestan, I lay marooned
In blistering heat, a bullet in my breast.
Smoke still rose in the valley from my wound
As drop-by-drop I watched blood flowing west.

I lay upon the loam of that strange land,
Cliffs closing in, the sun soon touching peaks,
Reaching past the mountain with its hand
To burn my dreaming brow and death-pale cheeks.

I dreamt I saw the flaming orb's bright glare
Feasting on poppies in my native parts,
And braided girls with flowers in their hair,
Recalling me with soft hands on their hearts.

But in the oaken table's hazy gleam
I saw another girl with half-crazed eyes.
She sat as if a captive in a dream,
Her stare the shade or shroud of starless skies.

She dreamt of that strange place in Dagestan,
Of smoke ascending over the black breast
Of a strange but somehow familiar man
As drop-by-drop he watched blood flowing west.

—*after the Russian of Mikhail Lermontov (1814-1841)*

PRZESZŁOŚĆ

1.
Nie Bóg stworzył p r z e s z ł o ś ć i śmierć, i cierpienia,
Lecz ów, co prawa rwie,
Więc nieznośne mu—dnie;
Więc, czując złe, chciał odepchnąć s p o m n i e n i a!

2.
Acz nie byłże jak dziecko, co wozem leci,
Powiadając: „O! dąb
Ucieka!... w lasu głąb..."
—Gdy dąb stoi, wóz z sobą unosi dzieci.

3.
Przeszłość jest i dziś, i te dziś daléj:
Za kołami to wieś
Nie—jakieś tam... coś, gdzieś,
Gdzie nigdy ludzie nie bywali!...

—*Cyprian Kamil Norwid (1821–1883)*

THE PAST

1.
God does not make the p a s t, nor death, nor grief,
But he who breaks the law,
Whose depths are so raw,
He, knowing evil, seeks a m n e s i a for relief.

2.
However, he's not like a child inside a stroller,
Crying: "Look, there's a tree,
Only to see it flee...
Into the woods!"; the tree remains; the child grows older.

3.
The past exists today as well as beyond the green:
A simple hamlet waits
Not this or that odd place...
Whose fields no living man has ever walked or seen.

—after the Polish of Cyprian Kamil Norwid (1821–1883)

ARCHAISCHER TORSO APOLLOS

Wir kannten nicht sein unerhörtes Haupt,
darin die Augenäpfel reiften. Aber
sein Torso glüht noch wie ein Kandelaber,
in dem sein Schauen, nur zurückgeschraubt,

sich hält und glänzt. Sonst könnte nicht der Bug
der Brust dich blenden, und im leisen Drehen
der Lenden könnte nicht ein Lächeln gehen
zu jener Mitte, die die Zeugung trug.

Sonst stünde dieser Stein entstellt und kurz
unter der Schultern durchsichtigem Sturz
und flimmerte nicht so wie Raubtierfelle;

und bräche nicht aus allen seinen Rändern
aus wie ein Stern: denn da ist keine Stelle,
die dich nicht sieht. Du musst dein Leben ändern.

—*Rainer Maria Rilke (1875-1926)*

APOLLO'S ARCHAIC TORSO

We have no knowledge of his ancient brow
where pippins ripen. Yet his torso gleams,
reflecting the candela, luminous streams
that yet pour from his gaze, his glance's glow

still radiant, though dimmed. If not, his bare
breast would not blind you in the silent turn
of hip and thighs, a smile not flash and burn
through groins, his genitals not ever glare.

If not, this stone would seem deformed and small,
the light beneath his shoulder's sudden fall
not seem a preying panther's shimmering mane,

not burst beyond the limits of the skies,
starlike, until there is no point or plane
blind to your ways. You must change your life.

—*after the German of Rainer Maria Rilke (1875-1926)*

CHWILA

Że mija? I cóż, że przemija?
Od tego chwila, by minęła.
Zaledwo moja, już niczyja,
Jak chmur znikome arcydzieła.

Chociaż się wszystko wiecznie zmienia
I chwila chwili nie pamięta,
Zawsze w jeziorach na przemiany
Kąpią się gwiazdy i dziewczęta.

—*Leopold Staff (1878-1957)*

THE MOMENT

What matter that it's passing? That it passes?
Moments exist if only to pass by,
Hardly mine, no longer anyone else's,
Like cloudy masterpieces in the sky.

Though everything perpetually changes,
And moments are replaced by moments waiting,
Always in lakes among the masterpieces
Either stars or pretty girls are bathing.

—*after the Polish of Leopold Staff (1878-1957)*

ASTERN

Astern—schwälende Tage,
alte Beschwörung, Bann,
die Götter halten die Waage
eine zögernde Stunde an.

Noch einmal die goldenen Herden,
der Himmel, das Licht, der Flor,
was brütet das alte Werden
unter den sterbenden Flügeln vor?

Noch einmal das Ersehnte,
den Rausch, der Rosen Du—
der Sommer stand und lehnte
und sah den Schwalben zu,

Noch einmal ein Vermuten,
wo längst Gewissheit wacht:
Die Schwalben streifen die Fluten
und trinken Fahrt und Nacht.

—*Gottfried Benn (1886-1956)*

ASTERS

Asters—sweltering days,
old entreaty, spell,
the gods shed timid rays,
an hour upon the scale.

Once more the golden flocks,
the sky, the light, the veil.
What breeds the familiar flux
of wings before they fail?

Once more now the lust,
the rush of roses, and you—
the summer's leaned to watch
the swallows skirt the dew,

and once more does not falter,
sure dark precedes new light:
the swallows drink the water
and fade into the night.

—after the German of Gottfried Benn (1886-1956)

LETZTER FRÜHLING

Nimm die Forsythien tief in dich hinein
und wenn der Flieder kommt, vermisch auch diesen
mit deinem Blut und Glück und Elendsein,
dem dunklen Grund, auf den du angewiesen.

Langsame Tage. Alles überwunden.
Und fragst du nicht, ob Ende, ob Beginn,
dann tragen dich vielleicht die Stunden
noch bis zum Juni mit den Rosen hin.

—*Gottfried Benn (1886-1956)*

LAST SPRING

Take the forsythias deep within, each leaf,
and when the lilac blossoms on the lawn,
mix it, too, with your blood and joy and grief,
the dark soil that you depend upon.

Sluggish days. All have been gotten through.
And if you do not ask: the start or close,
then perhaps the hours will carry you
as distantly as June's unfolding rose.

—*after the German of Gottfried Benn (1886-1956)*

EIN HERBSTABEND
An Karl Röck

Das braune Dorf. Ein Dunkles zeigt im Schreiten
Sich oft an Mauern, die im Herbste stehn,
Gestalten: Mann wie Weib, Verstorbene gehn
In kühlen Stoben jener Bett bereiten.

Hier spielen Knaben. Schwere Schatten breiten
Sich über braune Jauche. Mägde gehn
Durch feuchte Bläue und bisweilen sehn
Aus Augen sie, erfüllt von Nachtgeläuten.

Für Einsames ist eine Schenke da;
Das säumt geduldig unter dunklen Bogen,
Von goldenem Tabaksgewölk umzogen.

Doch immer ist das Eigne schwarz und nah.
Der Trunkne sinnt im Schatten alter Bogen
Den wilden Vögeln nach, die ferngezogen.

—*Georg Trakl (1887-1914)*

AN AUTUMN EVENING
To Karl Röck

The brown village. A darkness often treads
Along the walls that stand in autumn. Mock-
Shapes: man as well as woman, dead now, walk
In the cold parlours to prepare their beds.

Here young boys play. A heavy shadow spreads
Over brown dung. Servant women walk
Through the moist blue, and sometimes their eyes mock
It, longing, as bells toll above their heads.

An inn leans for the down and lonely there.
Patiently it waits beneath dark arches,
Moved by clouds of gold tobacco smoke,

Yet always black and near. A stranger soaked
In booze stands in the shade of older arches
After the wild birds take to the air.

—after the German of Georg Trakl (1887-1914)

НОЧЬ

Ночь, улица, фонарь, аптека,
Бессмысленный и тусклый свет.
Живи еще хоть четверть века—
Все будет так. Исхода нет.

Умрешь—начнешь опять сначала,
И повторится все, как встарь:
Ночь, ледяная рябь канала,
Аптека, улица, фонарь.

— *Алекса́ндр Бло́к (1888-1921)*

NIGHT

Night, street, lamp, and pharmacy,
A meaningless and misty light.
Live on a quarter century—
The same. There is no hope of flight.

You will die, rise from where you fell,
All be repeated, cold and damp:
The night, the wavering canal,
The pharmacy, the street, the lamp.

—*after the Russian of Alexander Blok (1888-1921)*

БЕРЕЗА

Белая береза
Под моим окном
Принакрылась снегом,
Точно серебром.

На пушистых ветках
Снежною каймой
Распустились кисти
Белой бахромой.

И стоит береза
В сонной тишине,
И горят снежинки
В золотом огне.

А заря, лениво
Обходя кругом,
Обсыпает ветки
Новым серебром.

— *Сергей Есенин (1895-1925)*

THE BIRCH

The birch beneath
My windowsill
Stands like a wreath
In the silver chill

Of winter, white
In the faint glow
Of early light
And softest snow.

The birch still yields
Stars at this time,
Though over fields
Sun breaks through rime.

Dawn wakes the grounds
And sleeping ploughs,
But makes its rounds
Through silver boughs.

—*after the Russian of Sergei Yesenin (1895-1925)*

DEZEMBER 1942

Wie Wintergewitter ein rollender Hall,
Zerschossen die Lehmwand von Bethlehems Stall.

Es liegt Maria erschlagen vorm Tor,
Ihr blutig Haar an die Steine fror.

Drei Landser ziehen vermummt vorbei.
Nicht brennt ihr Ohr von des Kindes Schrei.

Im Beutel den letzten Sonnblumenkern,
Sie suchen den Weg und sehn keinen Stern.

Aurum, thus, *myrrham offerunt...*
Um kahles Gehöft streicht Krähe und Hund.

...quia natus est nobis Dominus.
Auf fahlem Gerippe glänzt Öl und Ruß.

Vor Stalingrad verweht die Chaussee.
Sie führt in die Totenkammer aus Schnee.

—Peter Huchel (1903-1981)

DECEMBER 1942

How resounding is the winter squall.
Hole-riddled the loam walls of Bethlehem's stall.

That's Mary murdered at the entrance gate,
Hair frozen to the bloody stones and grate.

Masked in rags, three soldiers limping by
Cannot burn from her ear the infant's cry.

The last canteen sunflower won't get them far.
They seek the way and cannot see the star.

Aurum, thus, *myrrham offerunt...*
Crow and cur come to a manger ruined.

...quia natus est nobis Dominus.
On a bleached skeleton gleam soot and ooze.

The way to Stalingrad's a smouldering glow.
And it leads to a charnel house of snow.

—*after the German of Peter Huchel (1903-1981)*

ZABIJANIE RYBY

O czym płacze ta stara—ta pogryziona przez sole,
Ta biedna chorująca z petrunią—w kapeluszu?
I czemu tak się miota ta ryba na tym stole,
Pośród łamliwych szminek, rozsypanego różu?

I czemu tak wpatrzona ta stara w ową rybę,
Dlaczego tak pyszczkami chłeptają mdłe powietrze?
Dlaczego stare szminki są zeschłe i łamliwe,
A pudry coraz bledsze?

—*Stanisław Grochowiak (1934-1976)*

KILLING FISH

What's she crying about—this old crone eaten away by salt,
This poor sick woman with a petunia in her at two?
And why's this fish doing somersaults
Amid fragile lipsticks and scattered rouge?

And why does she keep staring at the fish like that,
What's its sickly mouth trying to tell her?
Why are old lipsticks fragile and cracked,
And powdered rouge paler and paler?

—after the Polish of Stanisław Grochowiak (1934-1976)

KOLĘDA

Schodzą powoli—tak złażą się, rzekłbyś—
Jedni oliwą po białka schlapani,
Inni z wielkimi krzywymi kciukami,
Wszyscy dziurawi jak gruzy lub rzeźby.

Baby... Te w ciasto spowite po łokcie;
Wdowy... Te w pudrze jak w śnieżnej zamieci;
Panny... Tak chude, że świeci szkielecik;
Płatne panienki—po trzynocnym poście.

Ze zwierząt koza, dwa gawrony, wielbłąd—
(Wielbłąd ze ZOO, ma przekłutą wargę),
Szpic ustrojony w spłowiała kokardę,
Kruk—jak w przepaskę—owinięty w bielmo.

Króle na końcu. Król w gazowym pysku,
Drugi ma gipsem zlutowane szczęki,
Trzeci jest jasny, jest nieomal piękny
W ostrej koronie z żelaznych odprysków.

I stoją. Patrzą. Matka między drzewa
Rozpięta—zwisa. Stopy się kołyszą,
Czasami kropla wstrząśnie martwą ciszą,
Czasem mysz ćwierknie lub kamień zaśpiewa.

A płód—Jak długo może drążyć ciało?
Jak długo gwiazda spada w naszych trzewiach?
Czasem mysz ćwierknie, czasem głaz zaśpiewa,
A to jest wszystko, co dotąd się stało...

—*Stanisław Grochowiak (1934-1976)*

CAROL

They come slowly—loiter, you might say,
Some with olive oil splashed on their bums,
Others with enormous crooked thumbs,
All full of holes like sculptures on display.

Broads...up to their elbows in sweet cake;
Widows...clad in blizzards of mock snow;
Ladies...so thin that their skeletons glow;
Tarts...with three nights of fasting in their wake.

Animals: a goat, two rooks, a camel,
(A camel from the ZOO with a pierced lip),
A spitz that wears a ribbon and a slip,
A raven perched on some strange nameless mammal.

The three kings last: one with a face of gauze,
The second with a jaw made out of plaster,
The third as beautiful as alabaster,
Though his crown's sharper than the teeth of saws.

They stand and watch. The mother, mid trees, swings,
Sprawled out, her feet rocking back and forth.
Sometimes a drop of silence hits the floor,
Sometimes a mouse squeaks, or a stone sings.

How long can the foetus keep flesh mired?
How long can the star fall in our marrows?
Sometimes a mouse squeaks, or boulder carols,
And this is all, so far, that has transpired...

—after the Polish of Stanisław Grochowiak (1934-1976)

CZARNE CZARNE GAWRONY

Czarne czarne gawrony dokąd stąd lecicie
Tutaj w moim ogrodzie krótkie wasze życie

Tutaj wokół karmnika tuż przy moich srokach
O gawrony! istnienia jaka czerń głęboka

I jakie wielkie dzioby i pazury mroczne
Tutaj w moim ogrodzie przepaście naoczne

Dla sikorek turkawek ja tu jestem obcy
O czym to ja myślałem kiedy byłem chłopcem

Myślałem że istnienie to będzie zabawka
Tuż przy moich wróbelkach turkawkach i kawkach

—*Jarosław Marek Rymkiewicz (1935-)*

BLACK, BLACK ROOKS

Black, black rooks, where, whence do you fly
Here in my garden how fast you die

Here near my feeder by my jays
O rooks! How being's blackness stays

And what dark claws and what great bill
Here in my garden the depths are real

For warblers and doves I am a riddle
What was I thinking when I was little

I thought being a toy amid hedgerows
Here by my sparrows, doves and crows

—after the Polish of Jarosław Marek Rymkiewicz (1935-)

NOTES ON THE POETS

NOTES

Considered Poland's greatest poet, **Adam Mickiewicz** was born into a family of Polish-Lithuanian nobles on 24 December 1798 (in what is today Belarus). Among his many masterpieces were a series of Petrarchan sonnets called *Sonety Krymskie* (1826), four of which I have translated and included in this book. He died on 26 November 1855 in Constantinople (now Istanbul), where he had gone to help organize Polish forces to fight against Russia in the Crimean War.

Descended from a Scottish officer who served in the Russian Army in the seventeenth century, literary fame came early to **Mikhail Lermontov** (born 15 October 1814) with the publication of a poem on Pushkin's death, which he blamed on the Russian legal system. For this, a soldier himself, he was court-martialled and sent to the Caucasus where he died on 25 July 1841 from a gunshot wound inflicted during a duel with another officer. The Dream, included in this collection, prophesies his demise with uncanny accuracy.

Cyprian Norwid (born 24 September 1821) grew up an orphan and was, by and large, self-taught. A highly talented man who could paint, draw and write with mastery, for a while he lived in New York City where he found work as a graphic artist. Much like Gerard Manley Hopkins, he was an innovator whose poems were re-discovered and appreciated only decades after his death. A loner and highly religious outsider, he died in Paris on 23 May 1883 in a hospice run by Polish nuns.

The most renowned and translated German-language poet of the 20th century, **Rainer Maria Rilke** was born in Prague on 4 December 1875. Well-travelled throughout Europe, in the final year of his life he praised Benito Mussolini in a letter to Aurelia Gallarati Scotti, describing Italian fascism as "a healing agent." Open-eyed, he died in the arms of his family doctor on 29 December 1926. The leukemia that killed him had been diagnosed late and had wreaked havoc on his body and mind.

One of the most accomplished and acclaimed Polish poets of the 20th century, **Leopold Staff** was born on 14 November 1878 in Lwów, Poland, (now Lviv, Ukraine.) Influenced by both the philosophy of Friedrich Nietzsche and the teachings of Saint Francis of Assisi, for most of his life he wrote rhymed metrical poems with the paradoxes of Christianity as their backdrop. He lived an emotionally stable life, unlike most poets, and died on 31 May 1957 at the age of 78.

Considered today the principle representative of Russian symbolism, **Alexander Blok** was born on 28 November 1880 in Saint Petersburg. Influenced by the writings of the mystical philosopher Vladimir Solovyov, he wrote poems in which sound and melody were of paramount importance. Although at first supportive of the Bolshevik revolution, he later grew disillusioned with it. On 7 August 1921, at age 40, he died in its wake, having suffered great hardship, both physical and mental, brought on, possibly, by venereal disease.

Gottfried Benn (born on 2 May 1886) used his experience in Imperial Germany's medical corps as the inspiration for his first two collections of poems. Written in free verse, they describe with great vividness his work specializing in the treatment of venereal disease. When the Nationalist Socialists came to power in Germany in the early 1930s, he praised and supported them, but by the late 1930s he fell out of favour and was not allowed to publish. At this point he wrote metrical poems, two of which I have translated and included in this book. After the war, he continued to write and publish, though disavowed by both the left and right. He died on 7 July 1956 in West Berlin.

Georg Trakl was born on 3 February 1887 in Salzburg, Austria. By age 15, he began drinking alcohol, and using opium, chloroform, and other drugs. At 18 he dropped out of school, preferring instead to work as a pharmacist's apprentice. In 1910 he joined the army for a three-year stint, after which he re-enlisted. In August 1914 he was an orderly dressing the heavy wounds of soldiers, sometimes as many as 90 a day. Unable to cope, he attempted to shoot himself in

Gródek (now in southern Poland), and was sent to a military hospital in Cracow for observation. On 3 November 1914 he administered himself an injection of cocaine resulting in a fatal overdose.

One of the most popular Russian poets of the 20th century, **Sergei Yesenin** was born on 21 September 1895. Encouraged and supported by established poets such as Alexander Blok, he began publishing early and received immediate recognition. A womanizer and heavy-drinker, he married four times (once to Isadora Duncan). After an alleged "mental breakdown" he was hospitalized by Soviet authorities for a month. Two days after his release (28 December 1925) he slit his wrists and, using blood as ink, wrote his final poem. He then hanged himself on heating pipes, or was hanged. The debate is still open.

Born near Berlin on 3 April 1903, **Peter Huchel** published his first poems in the 1930s while working for German radio. During World War II he served in the Luftwaffe until captured by the Red Army in 1945. After the war he worked for East German radio, and in 1949 became editor of *Sinn und Form*. Huchel grew out of favour with the communists soon after the Berlin Wall was built. Although forced into isolation, he was allowed to leave East Germany and settle in Rome. He died in West Germany on 30 April 1980.

Stanisław Grochowiak was born in Leszno, Poland on 24 January 1934. His first collection of poems was published in 1956 and was met with critical acclaim. Subsequent tomes and success followed. His style, classified as neo-Baroque, or neo-Metaphysical, was unique. (His contemporaries (Herbert, Rożewicz, and Szymborska) wrote free verse in the plain style, while Grochowiak reactivated rhyme and metre and employed conceits.) A heavy drinker, he died on 2 September 1976 in Warsaw.

Influenced by the both the Classist and Baroque traditions, **Jarosław Marek Rymkiewicz** (born on 13 July 1935) published his first book of poems in 1957. Today he is one of the leading Polish poets and critics, whose anti-communist and right-wing views have brought him into the public spotlight during a trial in which he was accused of libel for stating that the editor of Poland's leading newspaper was 'the spiritual heir' of the Polish communist party. He lives in Warsaw.

A POEM

BY

LEO YANKEVICH

LERMONTOV, VERLAINE, TRAKL, YESENIN

A bullet buried deep inside his breast,
Lermontov lay dead, but forever young.
The Paris sun descending in the west,
Verlaine slept with green absinthe on his tongue.

The wounded soldiers in the Polish mud
stalked Trakl to the kingdom in his vein.
His final poem written down in blood,
Yesenin dangled by the window pane.

Four poets lived, then perished by default
by either pistol, bottle, drug or noose.
(It burns to write lines worthy of one's salt.)

And whether by God's grace, gift, guile, or ruse,
each climbed Parnassus as in an assault,
and sang with cup and chain until let loose.

—Leo Yankevich, 11 May 2013

ABOUT LEO YANKEVICH

Leo Yankevich was born into a family of Roman Catholic Irish-Polish immigrants on 30 October 1961. He grew up and attended high school in Farrell, Pennsylvania, a small steel town in the Rust Belt of middle America. He then studied History and Polish at Alliance College, Cambridge Springs, Penn., receiving a BA in 1984. Later that year he travelled to Poland on a fellowship to study at the centuries-old Jagiellonian University in Krakow. A staunch anticommunist, he played an active role in the dissident movement in that country, and was arrested and beaten badly on a few occasions by the communist security forces. After the fall of the Iron Curtain in 1989, he decided to settle permanently in Poland. Since that time he has lived in Gliwice (Gleiwitz), an industrial city in Upper Silesia.

www.ingramcontent.com/pod-product-compliance
Lightning Source LLC
LaVergne TN
LVHW021624080426
835510LV00019B/2755